LEGO® STAR WARS™

RISE OF THE SITH

CONTENTS

INTRODUCTION

It is a time of peace for the glorious Galactic Republic. Its citizens have not known warfare in centuries. But the dark side is stirring. The ancient, evil Sith are not extinct as the Jedi believe.

Chancellor Palpatine, who is secretly an evil Sith Lord, controls the Republic. Through his dark side servants, he commands the Separatists to break away from the Republic, which leads to the catastrophic Clone Wars. Darth Sidious watches and knows that his victory is inevitable. No matter which side wins the Clone Wars, Sidious shall triumph – and the Jedi Knights will lose…

MWA HA HA! IT'S ALL GOING ACCORDING TO PLAN.

DARTH SIDIOUS

ALTHOUGH THE EVIL Sith are thought to be long gone, one has survived. Lurking behind the scenes, he has secretly manipulated the Republic, the Separatists and even the Jedi to fulfill his goals of conquest and revenge. To most, he is Palpatine… but his Sith name is Darth Sidious.

Eyes corrupted by dark side power

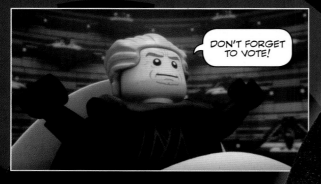

DON'T FORGET TO VOTE!

RISE TO POWER
At first, Palpatine appears to be a kind and humble senator from the planet Naboo. Through clever scheming, he is elected Chancellor of the entire Republic. Finally, he declares himself Emperor – the tyrannical leader of the new Galactic Empire!

EMPEROR PALPATINE
As Emperor, Sidious rules the galaxy through strength and fear. He does not care about crowns or fancy clothes, preferring to sit in the shadows and plot the destruction of all who oppose him. He does not believe that anything will ever topple his power.

A CRUEL MASTER

Being Sidious's Sith apprentice is not an easy job. The hard work, cruel punishments for failure and constant training are bad enough… but he's also always on the lookout for someone even stronger to replace you!

R-REALLY, MASTER – A WOOKIEE ATE MY HOMEWORK!

EVIL REVEALED

When the Jedi finally suspect Palpatine's true identity as a Sith Lord, they try to arrest him. Instead, Darth Sidious turns the tables and defeats them all – with the help of his newest apprentice, Darth Vader!

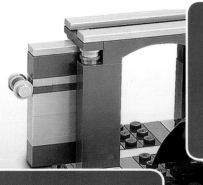

Force lightning

Chancellor's office

Jedi Master Mace Windu

Shadowy black robes

DATA FILE

- **HOMEWORLD:** NABOO
- **BIRTH DATE:** 82 BBY
- **RANK:** SITH LORD
- **TRAINED BY:** DARTH PLAGUEIS
- **WEAPON:** RED-BLADED LIGHTSABER, FORCE LIGHTNING

"EVERYTHING IS PROCEEDING AS I HAVE FORESEEN."
DARTH SIDIOUS

THE FORCE IS A mysterious, invisible energy that surrounds everything in the galaxy. The Sith follow the dark side of the Force, which teaches them to embrace anger, selfishness and power. The Jedi Knights follow the light side and learn calmness and compassion. Every Force user sees the Force differently!

THE FORCE IS PRESENT IN EVERY LIVING THING. IF WE LISTEN CAREFULLY, WE CAN LEARN FROM IT.

Qui-Gon Jinn believes in the Living Force.

THE FORCE CAN LET YOU SENSE DISTANT EVENTS AND FRIENDS, AND EVEN GLIMPSE THE FUTURE.

Yoda is one of the wisest and strongest Force users of all time.

THE FORCE BRINGS VICTORY IN BATTLE, AND PEACE AND JUSTICE TO THE GALAXY.

Mace Windu is a great warrior and lightsaber master.

THE FORCE IS KIND OF CONFUSING, BUT HANDY FOR GETTING OUT OF A JAM.

Luke Skywalker has much to learn about the Jedi path.

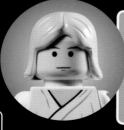

THE FORCE SHOULD BE USED WITH PATIENCE AND THOUGHTFULNESS.

Obi-Wan Kenobi is a disciplined and experienced Jedi.

THE FORCE

Followers of the **Unifying Force** philosophy believe that there is no real **light** side or **dark** side, but only different ways of **using** the Force.

POWER IS ALL THAT MATTERS, AND THE FORCE IS THE ULTIMATE SOURCE OF POWER.

Darth Sidious craves only one thing.

THE FORCE HELPS YOU KEEP THOSE AROUND YOU FRIGHTENED AND OBEDIENT.

Darth Vader wants order in the galaxy at any cost.

THE FORCE LETS YOU CONTROL THE MEEK, THE FOOLISH AND THE WEAK-WILLED.

Darth Tyranus manipulates others to serve his goals.

THE FORCE IS A TOOL FOR GETTING YOUR REVENGE.

Asajj Ventress is driven by rage.

THE FORCE LETS YOU BE BETTER THAN EVERYBODY ELSE.

Darth Maul always needs to win.

JEDI AND SITH
Which side of the Force is more powerful? The Sith believe that the dark side is stronger, and see the Jedi as weaklings. But while the dark side grants its users incredible strength, the Jedi train hard in the light side – and are often able to defeat a Sith who has chosen the quicker and easier path to power.

JEDI ORDER

Many **Sith** were once Jedi who **turned** to the dark side and **abandoned** the vows and teachings of the **Jedi Order**.

JEDI KNIGHTS
The Jedi are protectors of peace, but they are also skilled warriors who are ready to raise their lightsabers to combat evil. During the Clone Wars, Jedi Generals join forces to protect the Republic.

COLEMAN TREBOR

OBI-WAN KENOBI

SHAAK TI

HERE WE ARE, TO SAVE THE DAY!

AGEN KOLAR

KIT FISTO

BARRISS OFFEE

LUMINARA UNDULI

FOR TENS OF THOUSANDS of years, the Jedi Order has gathered together Force users from every intelligent species in the galaxy to safeguard harmony and justice. The Jedi are peacemakers, law keepers and defenders of those who cannot defend themselves. They are the greatest enemy of the dark side.

HOLOCRON VAULT
Inside the Jedi Temple on Coruscant is the fabled Holocron vault. Each Holocron information crystal contains a precious collection of Jedi knowledge. The Holocrons hold many centuries of the Order's history… and all of its secrets, too, making the Holocrons a much-desired prize for the Sith.

JEDI TECHNOLOGY
As protectors of the Republic, the Jedi fly starships that are built using the latest technology. Although some starfighters, such as Obi-Wan's Eta-2 Interceptor, are too small to be fitted with a hyperdrive of their own, the Republic have many hyperdrive rings, which can launch smaller ships into hyperspace.

DARK JEDI
Every so often, a Jedi may find himself tempted by the dark side. Jedi General Pong Krell has a dangerous craving for power – and he embraces the dark side to get it. During the Battle of Umbara, Krell sabotages his own troops to thwart the Republic's war effort. Such treachery allows Krell to join the ranks of other fallen Jedi, such as Count Dooku and Anakin Skywalker.

LET'S PUT OUR TROOPS RIGHT IN THE LINE OF FIRE.

UMM, OKAY...

Rare purple lightsaber blade

Wise and kindly face

Traditional Jedi robes

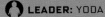

YODA

MACE WINDU

DATA FILE

LEADER: YODA

FOUNDED IN: 25,000 BBY

MISSION: PROMOTE PEACE AND PROTECT THE GALAXY

JEDI MASTERS
In the late days of the Republic, the two most important Jedi Masters are Yoda and Mace Windu. Although each has his own unique style of leading, both are committed to destroying the last remaining Sith. Unfortunately for them, the Sith strike first!

Head and body covered in tattoos

Zabrak horns

DATA FILE

🌐 **HOMEWORLD:** DATHOMIR

🏛 **BIRTH DATE:** 54 BBY

🛡 **RANK:** SITH LORD

👤 **TRAINED BY:** DARTH SIDIOUS

🗡 **WEAPON:** RED DOUBLE-BLADED LIGHTSABER

Darksaber of defeated Mandalorian leader

DARTH MAUL

SOMETIMES, THE SITH need to use cunning and subtlety. Other times, they just want a blunt instrument. Darth Maul may not be the most clever or sneaky of dark side warriors, but his strength and rage make him a huge danger to the Jedi – and the perfect first apprentice for Darth Sidious.

Cybernetic legs

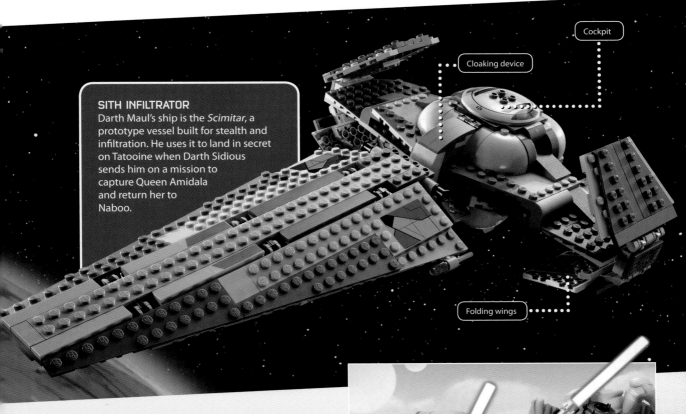

Cockpit

Cloaking device

Folding wings

SITH INFILTRATOR
Darth Maul's ship is the *Scimitar*, a prototype vessel built for stealth and infiltration. He uses it to land in secret on Tatooine when Darth Sidious sends him on a mission to capture Queen Amidala and return her to Naboo.

MAUL'S REVENGE
Even the loss of his entire lower body cannot put an end to Darth Maul. Years after his apparent death, he returns with a set of mechanical legs and takes over the planet Mandalore – until his rebellion is put to an end by his former Master, Darth Sidious.

> **"AT LAST WE WILL REVEAL OURSELVES TO THE JEDI. AT LAST WE WILL HAVE REVENGE."**
> DARTH MAUL

BOO! SURPRISE SITH ATTACK!

LOOK AT ME!
Darth Maul might have been defeated by the Jedi, but he is still a bit of a show off. After the destruction of the first Death Star, Darth Maul and Darth Vader find themselves competing for the Emperor's approval – and Maul can't resist demonstrating his awesome new eight-bladed lightsaber!

FIRST CONTACT
There has been no sign of the Sith for centuries – until now! When Qui-Gon Jinn travels to Tatooine with Obi-Wan and Queen Amidala, a sinister cloaked figure reveals himself as Darth Maul, an unknown Sith apprentice. Qui-Gon must act fast to protect Queen Amidala. He battles fiercely against the Sith, but only a well-timed jump into Amidala's starship saves the Jedi Master.

CAN A SITH APPRENTICE BE DEFEATED?

THE FULLY UNLEASHED power of the dark side has not been faced by the Jedi in many lifetimes. Now that Darth Maul has revealed himself, is there a Jedi in the galaxy who is brave enough to take a stand against his vengeful rage?

FEARLESS SITH
Darth Maul is a fearless warrior. He has used his powers of intimidation to help invade the peaceful planet of Naboo. When Jedi Master Qui-Gon Jinn and his Padawan apprentice, Obi-Wan Kenobi, confront Maul, he is more than ready to battle. To the surprise of his Jedi foes, Maul's lightsaber ignites with not one, but two deadly red blades.

A CLASH OF THE FORCE
Qui-Gon Jinn believes that the Force is an energy present in all living things. When laser walls separate Qui-Gon from Maul, the Jedi meditates to become one with the light side. Maul, eager to battle, paces impatiently, waiting for the walls to vanish. When the calm of the light side and the ferocity of the dark side come face to face, which will triumph?

C'MO-O-ON, LET'S FIGHT ALREADY!

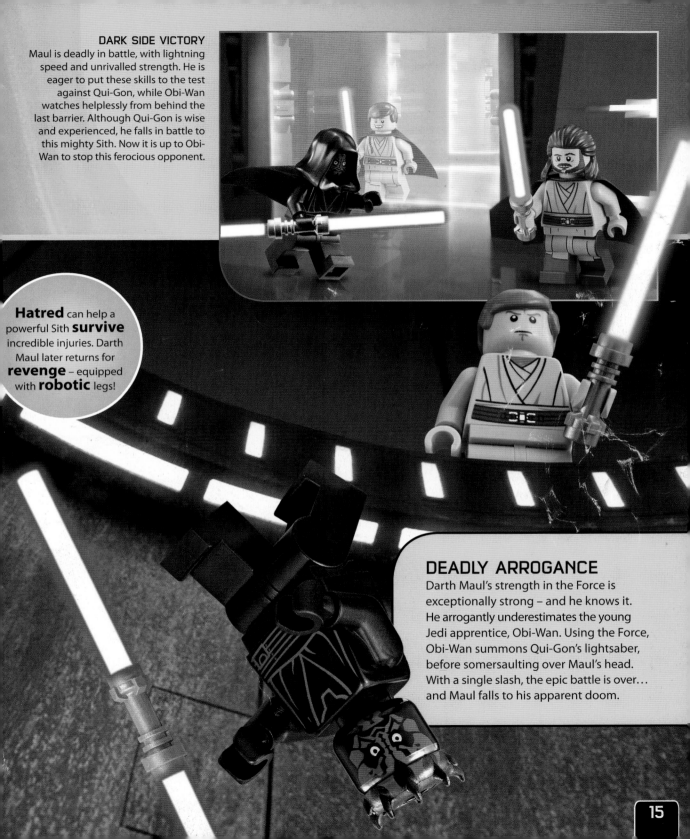

DARK SIDE VICTORY
Maul is deadly in battle, with lightning speed and unrivalled strength. He is eager to put these skills to the test against Qui-Gon, while Obi-Wan watches helplessly from behind the last barrier. Although Qui-Gon is wise and experienced, he falls in battle to this mighty Sith. Now it is up to Obi-Wan to stop this ferocious opponent.

Hatred can help a powerful Sith **survive** incredible injuries. Darth Maul later returns for **revenge** – equipped with **robotic** legs!

DEADLY ARROGANCE
Darth Maul's strength in the Force is exceptionally strong – and he knows it. He arrogantly underestimates the young Jedi apprentice, Obi-Wan. Using the Force, Obi-Wan summons Qui-Gon's lightsaber, before somersaulting over Maul's head. With a single slash, the epic battle is over... and Maul falls to his apparent doom.

DARTH TYRANUS

PUBLICLY KNOWN AS Count Dooku, Darth Sidious's second apprentice is a very different sort of Sith from Darth Maul. A born aristocrat and once a great Jedi Master, Tyranus is intelligent and charismatic, but with a streak of arrogance that leads him to quit the Jedi Order and join the dark side.

Handlebars control altitude

BEEP BEEP! IMPORTANT SITH COMING THROUGH!

Republic gunship in pursuit

Rear stabiliser fin

Forward-mounted driver's seat

GEONOSIS CHASE
Although he is supremely confident in his own abilities, Darth Tyranus is shrewd enough to retreat when his Master's plans demand it. As the Jedi arrive on the Separatist planet of Geonosis with their new Clone Army, Tyranus zooms away aboard his Flitknot speeder.

SEPARATIST LEADER
Using his well-known identity as the influential Count Dooku, Tyranus convinces unhappy members of the Republic such as the Geonosians and the Trade Federation to revolt against the Republic, starting the Clone Wars. Tyranus's Separatist allies believe he will lead them to victory, but it is secretly all part of a plot to give the Sith control over the galaxy.

THIS SEEMS LIKE A GOOD IDEA.

YES, A VERY GOOD IDEA!

Not only was Count Dooku a **respected** Jedi before he became a **Sith**, but he was also the teacher of Obi-Wan Kenobi's Master, **Qui-Gon Jinn**.

FOLLOWERS

Although he serves Darth Sidious loyally, Tyranus favours a leadership role. He trains the dark side assassin Asajj Ventress and supervises the reconstruction of the cyborg General Grievous. He even becomes the headmaster of a school for aspiring young Sith called "badawans!"

Elegantly trimmed facial hair

Cloak provides a hint of menace

DATA FILE

 HOMEWORLD: SERENNO

 BIRTH DATE: 102 BBY

 RANK: SITH LORD, FORMER JEDI MASTER

 TRAINED BY: YODA, DARTH SIDIOUS

 **WEAPON:** RED-BLADED LIGHTSABER

> ❝I'VE BECOME MORE **POWERFUL** THAN ANY **JEDI.**❞
> DARTH TYRANUS

Curved lightsaber hilt

FALLEN JEDI

As a Jedi, Count Dooku excelled at lightsaber fencing and moving objects with the Force, but he grew discontented with the Jedi Council and the Republic. As a Sith, Darth Tyranus cruelly enjoys deceiving his would-be friends and blasting his enemies with sizzling Force lightning.

WHAT HAPPENS WHEN A JEDI GIVES IN TO ANGER?

THE DARK SIDE is so powerful that even the strongest of Jedi Knights may have to work hard to evade its temptation. Jedi must learn to avoid negative feelings such as fear, anger and hate – or they may be pulled toward the dark side of the Force. What will happen when Anakin Skywalker, who has always had trouble controlling his emotions, gives in to his anger?

THE CAPTURED CHANCELLOR
Chancellor Palpatine is an excellent actor. He conceals his true Sith identity even from his closest allies. Palpatine fakes his own kidnapping, luring Anakin and Obi-Wan Kenobi to rescue him. When the Jedi finally track Palpatine down, he is imprisoned by Count Dooku, otherwise known as Darth Tyranus.

Darth **Tyranus** might have been in on Palpatine's kidnap **scheme**, but he certainly wasn't aware of what his **Sith Master** had planned for the finale.

A DEADLY DUEL
Tyranus's dark side powers make him a lethal opponent, and the Sith Lord takes on both Jedi at once. Sensing Anakin's rage and fear, Tyranus taunts him for not using those emotions to fight. Instead of focusing on the light side of the Force, Anakin begins to draw on his anger.

TYRANUS'S DOWNFALL
The dark side of the Force feeds on anger and hatred. As Anakin duels with increasing rage, he grows more and more powerful. From the sidelines, Chancellor Palpatine orders Anakin to destroy Tyranus. Anakin knows that a good Jedi would not give in to his rage, but he obeys the Chancellor… which is exactly what the devious Sith had planned all along.

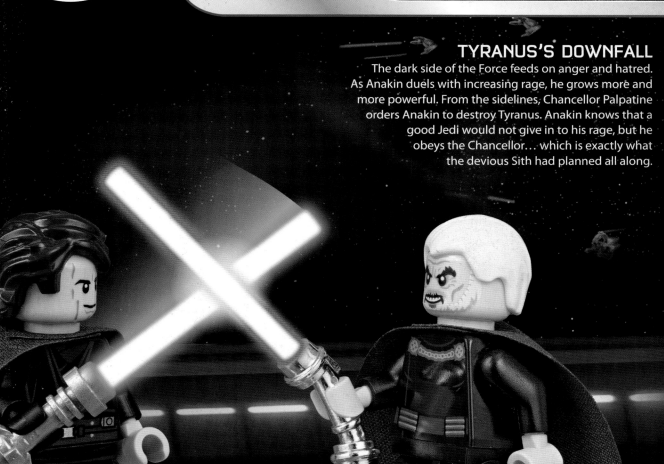

ORDER 66

ALL IS AS DARTH Sidious has planned. The Jedi Knights are scattered across the galaxy fighting in the Clone Wars, and Anakin Skywalker has sworn allegiance to the Sith as Darth Vader. Sidious sends a message to all the clone commanders: Execute Order 66 – the Jedi are traitors and must be destroyed!

I SENSE... DANGER!

UTAPAU
On the sinkhole planet Utapau, Obi-Wan Kenobi has just defeated the dreaded General Grievous when he is attacked by his own clone troopers under Commander Cody. Unlike most of the Jedi, Obi-Wan manages to escape the ambush.

SALEUCAMI
On Saleucami, Jedi Master Stass Allie is patrolling on her speeder bike with the loyal Commander Neyo. But when Neyo receives Order 66 from Darth Sidious, he turns his BARC speeder's lasers on his Jedi General.

THERE ARE BAD GUYS AROUND HERE SOMEWHERE...

EXECUTE ORDER 66.

FELUCIA
As she searches for enemy battle droids on the fungus-covered world of Felucia, Jedi Master Aayla Secura is struck down by the blasters of Clone Commander Bly and his fellow troopers of the 327th Star Corps.

JEDI TEMPLE
On Coruscant, Sidious commands Darth Vader to attack the Jedi Temple. Obedient to his new Master, Vader leads the 501st Legion to wipe out all the Jedi inside the Temple. The 501st Legion becomes Vader's personal battalion – and is later renamed "Vader's Fist."

CATO NEIMOIDIA
Jedi Master Plo Koon flies above the Separatist world of Cato Neimoidia in his Jedi starfighter. Although he is a skilled pilot, he is unprepared for his own squadron of ARC-170 starfighters to open fire on his ship from behind.

WHO WILL WIN: MASTER OR APPRENTICE?

FOR YEARS, ANAKIN SKYWALKER has studied the Jedi way under Obi-Wan Kenobi's expert guidance. But now he has fallen to the dark side and become a Sith. Will the newly renamed Darth Vader be strong enough to defeat and destroy his former friend and mentor?

THE JEDI ARE THE REAL BAD GUYS!

HAVE YOU LOOKED IN A MIRROR LATELY?

Lava skiff

MUSTAFAR CLASH
The volcanic world of Mustafar is a fiery, dangerous place. Obi-Wan follows Vader here to convince his former student to return to the side of good. But Vader's anger against the Jedi Order is far too great – and he declares Obi-Wan to be his enemy. Obi-Wan is left with no choice but to fight his old friend.

Like others who wield the **dark side** of the **Force**, Darth Vader's **hatred** and hunger for power cause his **eyes** to change to yellow and red.

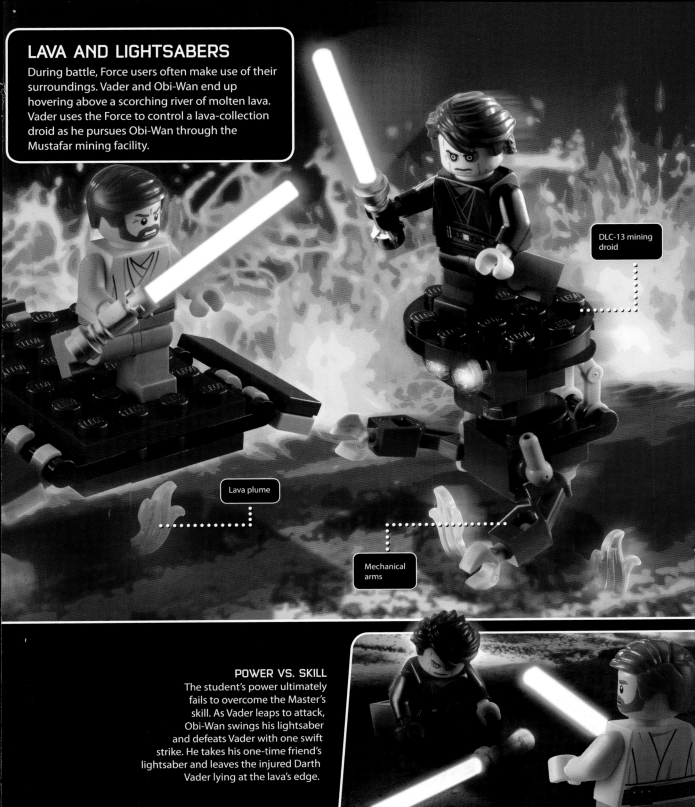

LAVA AND LIGHTSABERS

During battle, Force users often make use of their surroundings. Vader and Obi-Wan end up hovering above a scorching river of molten lava. Vader uses the Force to control a lava-collection droid as he pursues Obi-Wan through the Mustafar mining facility.

DLC-13 mining droid

Lava plume

Mechanical arms

POWER VS. SKILL
The student's power ultimately fails to overcome the Master's skill. As Vader leaps to attack, Obi-Wan swings his lightsaber and defeats Vader with one swift strike. He takes his one-time friend's lightsaber and leaves the injured Darth Vader lying at the lava's edge.

CAN A SITH LORD DEFEAT YODA?

DARTH SIDIOUS COMMANDS the dark side with such power that he fills his enemies with fear. But can this mightiest of Sith Lords defeat the Grand Master of the Jedi Order? Darth Sidious is eager to find out when Yoda challenges him to an incredible duel in the heart of the Senate building.

Despite all of his **Force** strength, even **wise** Yoda does not sense that Chancellor **Palpatine** is a Sith Lord – until it is **too late!**

THE NEW EMPEROR
Darth Sidious has transformed the Republic into an Empire! Yoda must take action, and fast, if he is to end the newly crowned Emperor's evil reign. Entering the Senate on Coruscant, Yoda finds his way blocked by the Emperor's Royal Guards. Wasting no time, Yoda effortlessly tosses them aside with the Force.

BLASTS OF POWER
Sidious deploys Force lightning with deadly skill. He sends a bolt of the crackling energy at Yoda, which hurls the tiny Jedi across the room. Yoda is stunned, but responds with a Force push of his own that sends the Emperor flying. When Sidious tries to get away, Yoda pulls out his lightsaber and challenges the Sith Lord to prove the dark side's power.

YOUR MATCH YOU HAVE FINALLY MET, SIDIOUS.

WE SHALL SEE, MY LITTLE GREEN FRIEND.

THE SENATE CHAMBER

Sith Lord and Jedi Master do battle atop the former Chancellor's podium. As it rises into the great Senate chamber, it is clear that that Sidious is not a match for Yoda's superior speed and agility. But he has another trick up his black-robed sleeve. With a mad cackle, he uses the Force to lift the chamber's floating Senate pods and throw them at Yoda. Yoda dodges the attack, and returns the favour, sending one pod flying right back at Sidious!

A MIGHTY FALL

Sidious is an agile Sith and is able to make a quick recovery. He blasts Yoda's lightsaber out of his hand and fires lethal lightning again. Yoda resists it, and the resulting Force explosion flings both fighters backward. Sidious catches himself, but Yoda plunges to the floor far below. Now it is the injured Jedi's turn to flee. Though his victory is only temporary, the Sith Lord stands triumphant!

MAN BECOMES MACHINE

DARTH VADER'S DUEL WITH Obi-Wan on Mustafar left him badly hurt. In order to save him, Darth Sidious – now Emperor Palpatine – calls on all the technology the Empire has to offer. His medical droids rebuild Vader's burned body with robotic parts, and cover his face with a black mask. He has become more machine than man.

Surgical Reconstruction Centre

THE SUIT MAY BE A LITTLE ITCHY, BUT YOU CAN'T EVER TAKE IT OFF.

Emperor Palpatine

BATTLE DAMAGE
Searing lava has scarred Vader's face and skin. Although he already had one mechanical arm, Obi-Wan's lightsaber has cost him the other one, along with both legs. Vader cannot even breathe on his own. Will his Master, Emperor Palpatine, find a way to keep him alive?

Mask contains respirator so Vader can breathe

NOOOOOOO!

MEDICAL DROIDS
No human can be trusted with repairing Sidious's prize. Vader's painful reconstruction is performed by two 2-1B surgical droids, a DD-13 "Chopper" droid and a multi-armed FX-6 assistant droid. The droids are not rewarded for their hard work; instead, the rebuilt Darth Vader crushes them with the power of the Force, fuelled by his rage.

Health-observing sensors

Life support and temperature monitors

Tools for cybernetic patients

FX-6 medical assistant droid

Angled operating table

SUIT OF ANGER
Anakin Skywalker was always a powerful Jedi. Now that he has fallen to the dark side, his power remains, but all traces of his old self are gone. Vader's new suit and mask enhance his strength and endurance. The suit also makes Vader feel enclosed and trapped. The Emperor is pleased to see his anguish and anger – he can use these emotions to turn Vader loose against the enemies of the Empire.

GLOSSARY

CHANCELLOR
The title given to the head of the Republic.

CLONE WARS
A series of galaxy-wide battles fought between the Republic's Clone Army and the Separatist Droid Army, which took place between 22 and 19 BBY.

CORUSCANT
The capital of the Republic – and later, the Empire. This planet is home to the Senate and the Jedi Temple.

CYBERNETIC
Something that is half mechanical, half biological.

CYBORG
A being that is partly a living organism and partly a robot.

DEATH STAR
An enormous Imperial battle station, which has enough firepower to destroy an entire planet.

EMPEROR
Ruler of the Empire.

EMPIRE
A tyrannical power that rules the galaxy under the leadership of Emperor Palpatine, a Sith Lord.

FORCE
The energy that flows through all living things. It can be used for good or evil.

FORCE LIGHTNING
Deadly rays of blue energy used as a weapon.

FORCE PUSH
A blast of energy that a Force-user can use to knock over an opponent.

HYPERDRIVE
A component in a starship that allows it to travel faster than the speed of light.

HYPERSPACE
An extra dimension of space, used by experienced starship pilots to travel faster than the speed of light using a hyperdrive.

JEDI
A member of the Jedi Order who studies the light side of the Force.

JEDI COUNCIL
Twelve senior Jedi who meet to make important decisions.

JEDI KNIGHT
A full member of the Jedi Order who has completed his or her training.

JEDI MASTER
An experienced and high-ranking Jedi who has demonstrated great skill and dedication.

JEDI ORDER
An ancient organisation that promotes peace and justice throughout the galaxy.

JEDI TEMPLE
The headquarters of the Jedi Order, located on the planet Coruscant.

LIGHTSABER
A sword-like weapon with a blade of pure energy that is used by Jedi and Sith.

LIVING FORCE
The view that the Force is present in all living things. Those who live by this view rely on their instincts and live in the moment.

ORDER 66
An order given by Chancellor Palpatine during the Clone Wars. Every clone trooper in the Clone Army was ordered to destroy all members of the Jedi Order.

PADAWAN
A young Jedi apprentice who is in training to become a fully fledged Jedi Knight.

REPUBLIC
The democratic government that rules many planets in the galaxy.

SENATE
The government of the Republic. It is made up of senators from all over the galaxy.

SEPARATISTS
An alliance of those who are opposed to the Republic.

SITH
An ancient sect of Force-sensitives who seek to use the dark side of the Force to gain power.

TRADE FEDERATION
A bureaucratic organisation that controls much of the trade and commerce in the galaxy.

Editors	**Shari Last and Matt Jones**
Designers	**Jon Hall and Rhys Thomas**
Additional Designers	**Julie Thompson and Mark Richards**
Senior DTP Designer	**David McDonald**
Senior Producer	**Lloyd Robertson**
Managing Editor	**Simon Hugo**
Design Manager	**Guy Harvey**
Creative Manager	**Sarah Harland**
Art Director	**Lisa Lanzarini**
Publisher	**Julie Ferris**
Publishing Director	**Simon Beecroft**

Additional photography by Gary Ombler.

Dorling Kindersley would like to thank Randi Sørensen and Robert Stefan Ekblom
at the LEGO Group; Jonathan W. Rinzler, Troy Alders, Rayne Roberts, Pablo Hidalgo,
and Leland Chee at Lucasfilm; and Jo Casey for editorial assistance.

First published in Great Britain in 2015 by
Dorling Kindersley Limited, 80 Strand, London, WC2R 0RL

Contains material previously published in LEGO® Star Wars™: The Dark Side (2014)

004-290606-Aug/15

Page design copyright © 2015 Dorling Kindersley Limited
A Penguin Random House Company

A CIP catalogue record for this book is available
from the British Library.

ISBN: 978-0-2412-4784-6

Printed in China

www.LEGO.com/starwars
www.starwars.com
www.dk.com

A WORLD OF IDEAS:
SEE ALL THERE IS TO KNOW